American Paintings from the Metropolitan Museum of Art

This exhibition is dedicated to the memory of
JAMES J. RORIMER
1905-1966

Library of Congress Catalogue Card No. 66-11293

❧ American Paintings from The Metropolitan Museum of Art ❧

Los Angeles County Museum of Art
Lytton Gallery
June 3 - July 31, 1966

M. H. De Young Memorial Museum
San Francisco
August 16 - October 16, 1966

⊰PREFACE AND ACKNOWLEDGMENTS⊱

During the past two decades, Californians have been given ample opportunity to know every nuance of the technical and stylistic development of post-World War II American art. They have responded with overwhelming enthusiasm in studying and collecting works of this period. They have had, however, little opportunity to develop an equal appreciation of the rich heritage of earlier American art. Consequently, the sponsors of this exhibition asked the Metropolitan Museum of Art to lend from its unparalleled American collection 125 paintings which exemplify the scope and quality of American art from the early eighteenth century to the first World War.

The response of the Metropolitan Museum staff far exceeded our expectations. The Director, James J. Rorimer, generously gave his time and advice in the initial planning of the exhibition. Associate Curator of American Painting and Sculpture, Stuart P. Feld, became the mainstay of the exhibition by providing wise counsel and reasoned professional judgment in the selection of works to be included. Associate Curators of American Painting and Sculpture, Albert Ten Eyck Gardner and Henry Geldzahler, made valuable contributions, each in his own area of specialization, and a score of staff members provided photographs and catalogue information and prepared the paintings for shipment, even completely restoring a number of them so they could be shown to best advantage. To all these, we are deeply indebted.

James Elliott, Chief Curator of the Los Angeles Museum of Art, and Alden S. Murray, Curator of Paintings at the de Young Museum served as members of the organization and selection committee, as did Larry Curry, Assistant Curator of American art at the Los Angeles County Museum of Art, who was responsible for the preparation of the catalogue. We would like to express our appreciation to the scores of anonymous museum personnel in all three institutions whose individual contributions were essential to the presentation of this exhibition.

Jack R. McGregor, Director
M.H. de Young Memorial Museum

Kenneth Donahue, Acting Director
Los Angeles County Museum of Art

⊰(TABLE OF CONTENTS)⊱

⟨INTRODUCTION⟩

In the seventeenth century the first settlers on the Eastern shores of America found the country in an almost pre-Columbian stage. Faced with the basic problems of survival, they showed an amazing capacity for self-government and self-discipline, and even as they struggled to provide themselves with the basic necessities of food, shelter and clothing, the pattern of a new culture began to evolve. In spite of rapid progress on the economic, social and political levels, over a hundred years passed before an artist could function. Because art is not utilitarian, it had to wait for the prevalent disposition to practicality to be softened somewhat by a period of relative ease and plenty. The Puritan's aversion to works of art had as much basis in his own daily life in the colonies as it had in the iconoclastic episode which took place in the Church of England. He probably objected not so much to the works themselves as to the wanton luxury or vanity which they might imply.

As the first colonies were being established in America the great Baroque painters of Europe were flourishing. Their art was a continuation of an unbroken tradition of several hundred years. The first American painters could not participate directly in European culture, and the sources of their art were secondary; yet, working in a new society in an isolated world, they proved equal to adversity. Their achievement is unique and, perhaps, not easy to understand. Early American works of art seem to invite generalization and simplification, so that their essential quality often escapes even the most competent critics. Some over-emphasize the naive or homespun factor, while others see only a provincial reflection of European art. The truth lies somewhere between these opposite views. Certainly, there is a somewhat forthright, rustic quality in some of the greatest examples of American paintings, as in the masterpieces of Winslow Homer, but Homer's work is a far cry from that of the primitive limner. The work of expatriates such as James McNeill Whistler, John Singer Sargent and Mary Cassatt is certainly derivative, but artists working here could never hope to emulate European painters to such an extent. Native artists who studied abroad usually had developed a distinctive personal style before departing; furthermore, they often came home disapproving of what they saw in foreign studios.

The development of the artistic tradition which was to provide the pictures for the homes of the early landowners and merchants was scarcely less difficult than the creation of the society itself. For a long time painting was limited to the efforts of the craftsman or artisan who painted or decorated coaches, gun carriages, fire buckets, funeral hatchments, signboards for inns or anything that wanted the touch of a skilled brush. When the demand for something approaching fine art arose, this man was the logical choice for the job, and whether he succeeded or failed depended largely upon his own ability. In order to achieve anything beyond the realm of primitive or folk art, aspiring artists had to find some source of instruction. Since there were no academies, they were forced to develop their art as best they could on their own, making use of the meager examples of European art available to them. A few of the more aristocratic settlers had brought with them to the New World treasured family portraits. These were extremely rare, however, and rarely seen by the native painters who could benefit from them. When artists from Great Britain and the Continent began to arrive in very limited numbers at the beginning of the eighteenth century, their advice and examples of their work were helpful to a few, but again, only a very few. Probably the most important sources of development for native artists in the eighteenth century the mezzotint engravings after English pictures which found their way to the colonies in increasing numbers. Often it is possible to match an American painting with the exact print which provided the basis for its composition.

When the colonist did begin to make use of the artist, the generally distrustful attitude toward art caused him to accept only the most practical form of art, the portrait. In the seventeenth and eithteenth centuries the American tradition of art was limited almost exclusively to portraiture, and the portrait continued to be the mainstay of the artist well into the nineteenth century. It was an extremely useful form of art as it was not only decorative, but documentary, perpetuating the image of the sitter for following generations of the family tree, and often indicating his station in life. Beyond mere practicality, however, there was a greater force operative in the primacy of face painting, that of cultural inheritance. The source of colonial painting was, after all, essentially that of England, where painting had been limited almost exclusively to portraiture since the Reformation. There, as in the colonies, religious subjects and ''fancy pictures'' were extremely rare. It was considered almost blasphemous for an artist, a mere human being, to attempt to depict the divinity inherent in the themes of the Scripture, and the creation of an image for the sole purpose of visual or esthetic pleasure was equally unthinkable.

As late as the Elizabethan period, Isaac Oliver and Nicholas Hilliard were still working in a Medieval tradition, painting their sitters in a flat, linear style which denied the existence of the third dimension or any suggestion of physical vitality. This tradition gave way only gradually as Anthony Van Dyck, Peter Lely and Gottfried Kneller arrived in England from the Continent to establish the Baroque style. Many of the early colonists coming from the outlying areas of England were undoubtedly familiar with the lingering Medieval style of the earlier Tudor period, and it had its effect on the first portraits of the New World. Very often, however, the influence of this Medieval quality is difficult to evaluate in specific pictures because it is so similar to the basic native element typical of works by the untrained artisan painters. At any rate, by the early eighteenth century when art began to attain more significance on the American scene, the major source of American painting was the Lely-Kneller style of the later period.

★ ★ ★ ★ ★

One of the earliest and most important exponents of the Knelleresque style in America was John Smibert. He arrived from England in 1729 with Bishop Berkeley who came to establish a College in Bermuda. The project failed and Smibert settled in Boston where his studio and ''colour shop'' (which he had to maintain to earn a living) became a center for the study of art. As important to the development of American painting as the artist himself and his work was his collection of prints and copies after the old masters, sought out and studied by such major figures as John Singleton Copley, Charles Willson Peale and Washington Allston. One of Smibert's more elaborate compositions, *Mrs. Francis Brinley and Her Infant Son* (no. 1c) includes standard devices of the period such as the window, urn and drapery. The picture is not as elegant as its English sources but the artist has achieved a rather firm grasp of character in the head of Mrs. Brinley. During the next hundred years, a keen insight into personality would be the salient quality of American portraiture.

Besides a number of artists largely unidentified portraying the families of the wealthy Dutch patroons of the Hudson, there were others who painted along the coast in the Knelleresque style: Henrietta Johnston and Jerimiah Theüs in Charleston, Charles Bridges at Westover, Justus Engel-hardt Kühn at Annapolis, Gustavus and John Hes-selius at Philadelphia, John Greenwood and Robert Feke at Boston and elsewhere. After Smibert's death in 1751, the principal artist working in Boston was Joseph Badger. A native born artisan whose trade was house and sign painting, he is typical of those who worked in isolation without the benefit of European experience. Though his art must have profited much from contact with Smibert and famil-iarity with that artist's work, he was unable to ad-vance much beyond the level of primitive limner. Primitivism need not imply inferiority, however, and in an occasional portrait such as that of his grandson James Badger, (no. 2) his sensitivity and directness tend to compensate for the obvious faults.

In London, the years following the death of Gottfried Kneller in 1723 saw the waning of the Baroque and the emergence of the elegant, more delicate Rococo style. This new taste, established in the art of William Hogarth, Thomas Hudson and Joseph Highmore, was soon reflected in the colonies in the work of such artists as Joseph Blackburn and John Wollaston. Blackburn's por-trait of *Mary Sylvester as a Shepherdess* (no. 3) is strongly indicative of a London background and his preoccupation with elegant forms of ribbons, flowers, jewelry and ruffles marks a distinct de-parture from the style of Smibert. As important as this new example was to be to the native artist, however, its assimilation took time, and the old manner lingered on. A case in point is John Hes-selius, son of Gustavus Hesselius who had brought the Baroque formula to Philadelphia as early as 1711. He was among those who eagerly adopted the fashionable style of Wollaston, yet from time to time he reverted to a rather stark, simple image as in the portrait of the austere *Mrs. Richard Gal-loway* (no. 4).

By the middle of the eighteenth century, the stage was set for the culmination of native painting in the art of John Singleton Copley and Benjamin West. The ever increasing demand for portraits which was the basis of success for Blackburn and Wollaston, now made art a very profitable en-deavor. Indeed, Copley could devote all his time to the development of his art and become wealthy in the process. There was much more involved in his great success, however, than mere supply and demand. The quality of his great work reflects, more than anything else, his native genius, and as the cultural soil of America became gradually more fertile, this genius was bound to flower. In terms of sources, his experience was not unique. He made use of prints and pictures generally available in the colonies, but he was to some extent privi-leged in this respect, in that his step-father was the English trained engraver, Peter Pelham. When Blackburn arrived in Boston in 1754, there was no one better equipped than Copley to understand his work. He quickly absorbed the new London manner of this artist and surpassed him. In *Joseph Sherburne* (no. 5c), his great gift for composition, his firm, sure sense of form and light and his grasp of character are clearly demonstrated. The portraits of this period would have in themselves established him as a major figure in the history of art, but he was not satisfied. In 1774 he sailed for Europe to begin a new career.

It was inevitable that truly accomplished and devoted artists such as Copley and West would be-gin to feel the restrictions inherent in the Ameri-can scene. After a time prints and the example of lesser artists from London were no longer useful to them as a source of real instruction, and the strict adherence to the portrait as the only legiti-mate subject began to pall. To be the best artist in America was simply not enough. The standard books on the theory and practice of art afforded them a tantalizing glimpse of the grand tradition of Euro-pean painting, which dealt with the great subjects of history, mythology and religion. Realizing that in America they could never approach this sub-lime realm of art they were compelled to travel to its source, to England and the Continent.

Benjamin West was the first American to study abroad. Arriving in Rome in 1760, he immediately began a program of study which was to make him an acknowledged leader of painting in the grand style. Here, he came into contact with the ideas of the German scholar Winckelmann and the artist Anton Raphael Mengs who emphasized the Antique as the basis for all artistic endeavor. He enjoyed considerable popularity, and gained access to all the great collections in Italy. In 1763, he settled in London, where, with the patronage of George III, he was to be a dominant figure for the rest of his life. In 1772, the King appointed him royal history painter and in 1792 he became president of the Royal Academy, which he had been instrumental in establishing only five years after his arrival. Thus, the phenomenal transformation of the American colonial into a powerful arbiter of European taste, was complete in a remarkably short time. Given the happy combination of the artist's genius and such ideal circumstances, it is no wonder that he was ahead of his time. In the thoroughly classical *Return of the Prodigal Son* (no. 6C) painted about 1771, he already anticipated the Neo-classicism of Jacques Louis David in France.

If West was important in Europe, his role in the development of American art was more significant. As other colonial artists came to England seeking instruction, he received them with great generosity. His studio became in effect an American school in London. Among those who studied or worked with him were John Singleton Copley, Charles Willson Peale, Ralph Earl, Henry Benbridge, John Trumbull, Mather Brown and Rembrandt Peale—in fact, a great percentage of the artists represented in the present exhibition. Thus, America gradually gained a strong nucleus of trained artists more familiar with the historical bases of their profession. They did not come home transformed, nor did they all become history painters. Portraiture continued to be the business at hand, and commissions were sought wherever available, their works reflecting the results of their training in varying degrees. The works of Charles Willson Peale, Henry Benbridge and Ralph Earl seem less affected by the English experience than those of the expatriate Mather Brown, or John Trumbull. Gilbert Stuart, who spent altogether more than fifteen years in Dublin and London became the great master of the Georgian portrait in America. His proficiency is clearly apparent in such works as *Man in a Green Coat* (no. 14) and the Phillips-Brixey *George Washington* (no. 17C).

* * * * *

The first years of the nineteenth century saw an increasing expansion of the visual arts in the youthful nation. Museums and public collections were formed and the establishment of the American Academy of Fine Arts, and the Pennsylvania Academy of Fine Art, seemed to confirm the prestige which the profession had attained. Prospects for the young artists were growing brighter at home, but a greater cultural awareness made them all the more anxious to study across the sea. The standard ''grand tour'' of European galleries and the pilgrimage to London continued well into the century.

Standing as a bridge between the eighteenth and nineteenth centuries is the work of Thomas Sully, who adhered to the Georgian portrait formula more closely than any of his contemporaries. His style was based on the romantic portraits of Thomas Lawrence, which he studied carefully in London. The fluid brushwork and the intense subjectivity of *The Student* (no. 19C) indicates how brilliantly he succeeded in assimilating Lawrence's manner. This kind of romanticism was typical of the period, but in the hands of most of Sully's generation, it became tempered with an increasing tendency toward naturalism. Expression varied from the keenly observed, spontaneous portrait of *Alexander Anderson* (no. 21) by John Wesley Jarvis to the more or less overtly romantic but descriptive works of Henry Inman, Samuel F. B. Morse, Chester Harding and the immigrant painters, Charles Ingham and William Hubard. Toward the middle of the century portraiture began to wane as the painter gave ground in this field to the photographer. The evolution which took place can be clearly demonstrated in a comparison of Samuel Waldo's vital, expressive portrait of *General Andrew*

Jackson (no. 27) with the rather workmanlike depiction of *The Knapp Children* (no. 28), painted in collaboration with his assistant, William Jewett.

West's history painting in the grand manner could not be transplanted to the rugged soil of America. John Trumbull was moderately successful because he depicted America's own history, the exploits of the Revolution, and his work set a precedent for military painting which dealt in turn with the War of 1812, the Mexican War and the Civil War. But those who were determined to imitate the great machines of London and Paris were doomed to bitter failure. Washington Allston expended his energy on the great *Belshazzar's Feast* (Detroit Institute of Fine Arts) which was never finished, and Rembrandt Peale struggled for years with his enormous *Court of Death* (Detroit Institute of Arts), but was forced in the end to concentrate on repetitions of his famous "porthole" portrait of *George Washington* (no. 30). If history painting could not succeed, however, it could provide the impetus for another significant development. In the hands of Washington Allston the incipient romanticism of Neo-classicism was given full expression, and in his work the Romantic tradition of the nineteenth century is begun. In *The Spanish Girl in Reverie* (no. 32), he was actually painting his own reverie, for he had never been to Spain, and the intensely evocative quality of the picture arises entirely from his powerful imagination. Compared to *The Wages of War* (no. 33) by Henry Peters Gray who continues a rather sentimental nostalgia for classical grandeur, Allston's work becomes all the more significant.

★ ★ ★ ★ ★

During the second quarter of the nineteenth century the face of America was being rapidly transformed. It was the age of Jacksonian Democracy and the "rise of the common man", who proved to be a rugged, self-reliant individual. As technological advance revolutionized industry, transportation and agriculture, an ever expanding increasing population moved westward, pushing relentlessly against the wilderness. In a very real sense, Americans were discovering America, and a spirit of optimism pervaded the land. Expansion and diversification extended into every aspect of life, including the visual arts. In 1826 a disgruntled band of students broke away from the American Academy of Fine Arts and under the leadership of Samuel F. B. Morse founded the National Academy of Design. In this much more vital institution, a program of annual exhibitions was initiated, making pictures generally more accessible to the public and students alike. Artists still toured Europe, but toward the middle of the century Dusseldorf became the great center for study. The proliferation of prints and illustrated instruction books now made it possible for one to achieve a professional level in painting without academic training. Landscape and genre painting evolved rapidly, with landscape replacing portraiture in order of importance.

In the eighteenth century, landscape was little more than a form of amusement for portrait painters, and their "landskips", adhering to a traditional formula, had little to do with nature. The nineteenth century artist approached nature directly and saw it as the manifestation of pure life force or divine will. The image which he produced was at once extremely romantic and realistic, a sensitive response to the drama of American scenery based on careful observation at times verging on the scientific. The artists who accompanied the expeditions to the great West or travelled beyond the frontiers alone often functioned as naturalists, reporting all the wonders which this land had to offer, but many of them such as George Catlin and Alfred Jacob Miller brought back works of great esthetic significance. John James Audubon tramped the wilderness alone for long periods studying the birds and animals of America at first hand. The *Ivory-billed Woodpeckers* (no. 34) is typical of his enormous production. The spirit of his work is carried on in the work of the animal painter, Thomas Hewes Hinckley, whose *Rabbit Hunting* (no. 35) includes elements of genre and landscape.

Great distances did not need to be covered, however, in order to find great scenery. The Hudson

Valley provided some of the most inspiring views to be found anywhere in the world, and as steamboat traffic on the river increased, it became readily accessible. By the second decade artists trained as engravers (as was often the case) began to publish portfolios of views in series. These tended to be rather formal and topographical in nature, like the later *View of the Bay and City of New York . . .* (no. 36) by Robert Havell, but by the third decade the major pioneers of the landscape movement Thomas Cole and Asher Brown Durand, had begun to set the historical standards of the "Hudson River School."

Both Cole and Durand worked first as engravers, and travelled in Europe where they were more inspired by the landscape than by the antique sculpture which had been the basis of study in the past. Cole's *The Voyage of Life* and similar allegorical subjects painted in series after his first trip abroad are among the most important monuments of Romantic art in America, and the expressive power of these works carries into his depiction of landscape. In *The Mountain Ford* (no. 38c) he creates an almost Wagnerian mood, yet no poetic generalization obscures the essential quality of the wild mountain scenery. Similarly, Durand's magnificent picture, *The Beeches* (no. 39c) remains faithful to nature, but the golden, almost ethereal light pervading the atmosphere is not a natural phenomenon. It derives in fact from the work of Claude Lorrain whose paintings Durand studied in the galleries of Europe. During the following years, other artists involved in this movement, notably John Kensett, Worthington Whittredge and Sanford Gifford developed an intense interest in the observed effects of sunlight, with the result that their work became increasingly naturalistic. Unlike the French Impressionists, however, they were not interested in the physical analysis of light as such. Their response to nature remained essentially subjective as they sought to capture the poetic or dramatic luminosity of their subject.

The latter half of the nineteenth century saw some significant changes in the tradition of landscape. Although the "Hudson River School" continued, the Hudson Valley itself became less important as a center of interest. Artists began to look further afield, and as the Far West opened up they could not resist the lure of its great mountains and endless plains. Among the foremost painters recording the splendor of this area were Albert Bierstadt, Thomas Moran and William Keith. The great dramatic impact of Bierstadt's *Merced River, Yosemite Valley* (no. 45c) reflects not only his German background and training at Düsseldorf, but also a reaction to nature which seems peculiarly American. In the art of Frederic Church and Martin Johnson Heade, naturalism becomes the dominant concern. Inspired by the books of the great German naturalist, Alexander von Humboldt, Church decided to catalogue all the various kinds of scenery around the world, and in carrying out this program, he visited Colombia, Equador, Labrador, the West Indies, Europe and the Near East. As these expeditionary artists became more ambitious the scale of their canvasses expanded in proportion, encompassing more and more of the world.

★ ★ ★ ★ ★

Still life painting has never been as prevalent in America as portraiture, landscape, narrative painting or genre; yet, in spite of this, it is not without importance. Since there was little demand for this branch of painting, the artists who indulged in it were usually working to satisfy their own esthetic standards. Like landscape and portraiture, still life can be either romantic or realistic, either subjective or objective, but hardly ever idealistic in the sense of serving a great human purpose; therefore, it is significant that some of the finest examples of this art were produced by the Peale family as early as the second decade of the nineteenth century when classical antiquity was just giving way to nature as motivation for art. In spirit and in quality, James Peale's *Still Life: Balsam Apple and Vegetables* (no. 50c) has much in common with some of the best of the early landscapes.

Evolving almost simultaneously with landscape,

genre painting celebrated the common man of Jacksonian democracy. In the works of artists such as George Caleb Bingham, William Sidney Mount and Richard Caton Woodville, three of the major exponents of the school, almost every aspect of daily life is portrayed with great affection and understanding. These artists understood their subject well, because they were themselves products of the new democracy. Many of them were essentially self-taught, relying heavily on good sound draughtmanship and the laws of traditional composition set forth in the instruction books of the period. In the latter half of the century the genre style became generally more atmospheric and realistic as the impact of European training began to register. This painterly manner is typical of the later works of Eastman Johnson, John G. Brown, Henry Mosler, Frank Waller and Edward L. Henry. In John Ferguson Weir's *Forging the Shaft* (no. 60C), an unusual industrial subject, the artist has performed a remarkable feat in realizing the effect of firelight penetrating a vast gloomy interior. Here, the expansiveness of depicted space is directly related to the ample dimensions of the canvas, and in this respect the picture is typical of the later nineteenth century. Like the artists Bierstadt and Church, the genre painters increased the size of their pictures to give them more scope and to more closely approach the actual scale of their subject. The figures in Thomas Hovenden's *The Last Moments of John Brown* (no. 63), become all the more real as they approach life size.

The culmination of realism occurs in the art of Winslow Homer and Thomas Eakins. No other artists in the history of American painting, except perhaps the *trompe l'oeil* painters, William Harnett and John Peto, have been less concerned with style as such or more intent upon setting down the appearance of nature as it meets the eye. Both studied in Europe, but a spirit of independence caused them to reject any influence which did not serve their purpose. This is not to imply, however, that they were completely alike. Of the two, Homer was given more to generalization, but within the broad design of his works he did not neglect the the subtle nuance of light and tone, so that even a small picture such as *Snap the Whip* (no. 65C) attains a monumental quality. An earlier composition, *The Veteran in a New Field* (no. 66) becomes almost a tour de force of simplicity. Eakins shared this tendency toward bold simplicity, but his approach differed considerably. To him, the mind was more important than the eye, and his art has its basis in a thorough program of scientific inquiry. A modern Leonardo, he made good use of the technology available to him, attending medical school to perfect his knowledge of anatomy and devising his own camera to record the human figure in motion. As a teacher at the Pennsylvania Academy, he insisted on the use of a nude model. The painterly quality of his earlier work, exemplified in *Pushing for Rail* (no. 68C), derives in part from his careful study of Ribera and Velasquez in Spain, and this quality continues in some of his most articulate anatomical studies such as *Arcadia* (no. 69).

The culmination in the art of Homer, Eakins and the "fool the eye" painters, Harnett, and Peto, was accompanied by the ultimate development of romanticism at the other end of the spectrum. The withdrawal from the real world begun by Allston progressed in the works of John Quidor and Elihu Vedder whose subjects are often remote in time and alien in spirit. By the last decade of the nineteenth century, Ralph A. Blakelock and Albert P. Ryder were completely committed to the mystery of the inner mind. In the case of these artists, however, tradition must not be over-emphasized, for they are essentially dreamers who invent their own world and make art conform to it. While ostensibly painting a landscape, Blakelock could spend months scraping, rubbing and brushing the surface of his picture, searching and hoping for the elusive quality of his private vision, and in the same way Ryder lived with his pictures for long periods repainting and reworking them as his inspiration dictated. Working with a wider range of subjects, Ryder is the more versatile of the two and seems to have greater depth. In his *Forest of Arden* (no. 77) he achieves an image which is at once timeless and enigmatic.

More isolated than Ryder or any of the most thorough independents of the American tradition is the primitive or naive painter. Divorced from tradition, he depended on nothing more than his innate talent and his proficiency as a craftsman. Generally, he did not make use of instruction books, and if he copied the work of a professional artist, he treated it the same way as a living subject, fixing on the most salient features which could be transcribed most easily and systematically. His art is varied but it does not develop in a cumulative, historical sense. Working under similar limitations, the ''Unknown Hudson Valley Painter'', who portrayed the *Young Lady with a Rose* (no. 78) has much in common with Edward Hicks, the author of a tribute to nature a hundred years later in *The Falls of Niagara* (no. 83c).

★ ★ ★ ★ ★

Toward the end of the nineteenth century American artists went to Europe in increasing numbers. In the seventies, the center was Munich where Frank Duveneck and William Merritt Chase developed their characteristic style based on slashing brushwork and a sombre palette. During the eighties and nineties interest was centered in Paris. Those who studied there during this period, however, were by no means setting a precedent. As early as the fifties, William Morris Hunt had returned to Boston expounding the doctrine of Jean Francois Millet and the Barbizon painters, and found to his surprise that their pictures were already being imported there. This school had a considerable influence in the early work of John La Farge, and other artists who had been associated with the Hudson River School, including Samuel Colman, Alexander H. Wyant and George Inness. The late works of Homer D. Martin and Inness began to reflect the impact of Impressionism, but in a very conservative, and personal way. The great expatriates of this period, James McNeill Whistler, Mary Cassatt and John Singer Sargent absorbed the best that Paris had to offer in terms of training and experience, and took their place among the first rank of European artists. Whistler, always the romantic, transformed the elements of Impressionism within his own personal style while Cassatt followed more closely the examples of her friend Edgar Degas. In the studio of Carolus-Duran, Sargent developed a direct, broad stroke that was to serve him throughout his life. Childe Hassam, Julian Alden Weir, John Henry Twachtman, Thomas Wilmer Dewing and others returned to America with an Impressionist style that was to carry well into the twentieth century.

The overwhelming influence of European teaching in the last years of the nineteenth century made American art almost more provincial than it had been even in Colonial times, and by the turn of the century the National Academy had become a bastion of conservatism reflecting the lessons of Gerome, Fortuny and Bonnat. This was the situation confronting the Eight Group, Robert Henri, William Glackens, George Luks, John Sloan, Everett Shinn, Ernest Lawson, Maurice Prendergast and Arthur B. Davies, as they emerged to begin their assault on public taste. The dream-like landscapes and figures of Davies are essentially romantic, and in the works of Lawson and Prendergast, Impressionism lingers on. The other five of their number, especially Henri, Luks and Sloan, were the real radicals. Having trained at the Pennsylvania Academy under Eakins's successor, Thomas P. Anschutz, they were well grounded in the realism of the nineteenth century. In New York, this tradition was applied to a new kind of subject matter, the crowded slums of the lower East Side. It is ironic that Arthur B. Davies, the most conservative of the group, was to be the principal organizer of the great Armory Show of 1913 in New York which introduced twentieth century European Art and revolutionized American painting.

LARRY CURRY

⊰ EXPLANATORY NOTES ⊱

In the text and index, catalogue numbers followed by the letter ''c'' refer to pictures reproduced in color.

In dimensions given, height precedes width.

◄[2]►
JOSEPH BADGER, 1708-1765
James Badger
Dated 1760
Oil on canvas, 42½ x 33⅛″
Rogers Fund, 1929

➤❲ 3 ❳◄

JOSEPH BLACKBURN (active in America 1754-1763)
Mary Sylvester
Painted about 1754
Oil on canvas, 49⅞ x 40-3/16″
Gift of Sylvester Dering, 1916

⇥❨ 4 ❩⇤

JOHN HESSELIUS, 1728-1778
Mrs. Richard Galloway, Jr.
Dated 1764
Oil on canvas, 36¾ x 30″
Maria De Witt Jesup Fund, 1922

❧ 7 ❧

BENJAMIN WEST, 1738-1820
Omnia Vincit Amor, or The Power of Love in the Three Elements
Painted about 1811
Oil on canvas, 70⅜ x 80½"
Maria De Witt Jesup Fund, 1923

⊰ 8 ⊱

CHARLES WILLSON PEALE, 1741-1827
Mrs. Samuel Mifflin and Her Granddaughter Rebecca Mifflin Francis
Painted in 1777-1780
Oil on canvas, 49¾ x 39¾"
Egleston Fund, 1922

❧ 9 ❧

HENRY BENBRIDGE, 1744-1812
Mrs. Benjamin Simons II
Painted about 1771-1773
Oil on canvas, 29⅞ x 25″
Fletcher Fund, 1929

❧{ 10 }❧
RALPH EARL, 1751-1801
Mrs. Noah Smith and Her Children
Dated 1798
Oil on canvas, 63¾ x 85¾″
Gift of Edgar William and Bernice Chrysler Garbisch, 1964

❧{ 11 }❧

UNKNOWN PAINTER
Jonathan Dwight I
Painted about 1790-1800
Oil on canvas, 29½ x 26¼"
Gift of Barbara Mercer Adam and Charlotte Adam Coate, 1961

❧ 1 2 ❧

MATHER BROWN, 1761-1831
Lady with a Dog
Dated 1786
Oil on canvas, 49½ x 39½"
Bertram F. and Susie Brummer Foundation, Inc., Gift, 1964

⊰ 13 ⊱

JOHN TRUMBULL, 1756-1843
Alexander Hamilton
Oil on canvas, 30¾ x 24¾"
Gift of Henry G. Marquand, 1881

❧{ 14 }❧

GILBERT STUART, 1755-1828
Man in a Green Coat
Painted about 1780-1785
Oil on canvas, 28½ x 23½"
Bequest of Mary Stillman Harkness, 1950

❖❨ 1 5 ❩❖

GILBERT STUART, 1755-1828
Matthew Clarkson
Painted about 1794
Oil on canvas, 36⅛ x 28¼″
Bequest of Helen Shelton Clarkson, 1938

◄ 16 ►

GILBERT STUART, 1755-1828

Ann Penn Allen

Painted about 1795

Oil on canvas, 29 x 24″

Bequest of Richard de Wolfe Brixey, 1943

⊰│ 18 │⊱

THOMAS SULLY, 1783-1872
Mrs. Katherine Matthews
Painted in 1812-1813
Oil on canvas, 27⅜ x 23⅛″
Rogers Fund, 1906

[20]

THOMAS SULLY, 1783-1872
The Rosebud
Dated 1841
Oil on canvas, 23⅞ x 36½″
Bequest of Francis T. S. Darley, 1914

⊰(21)⊱

JOHN WESLEY JARVIS, 1780-1840
Alexander Anderson
Painted in 1815
Oil on canvas, 34 x 27″
Gift of Robert Hoe, 1881

❧ I ❧

JOHN SMIBERT, 1688-1751
Mrs. Francis Brinley and Her Infant Son
Painted about 1731
Oil on canvas, 50 x 39¼″
Rogers Fund, 1962

❧(22)❧

HENRY INMAN, 1801-1846
William Charles Macready
Painted about 1827
Oil on canvas, 30¼ x 25"
Rogers Fund, 1906

❦〔 2 3 〕❦
SAMUEL FINLEY BREESE MORSE, 1791-1872
Mrs. Daniel De Saussure Bacot
Painted about 1820
Oil on canvas, 30 x 24¾″
Morris K. Jesup Fund, 1930

◄[5]►

JOHN SINGLETON COPLEY, 1738-1815
Joseph Sherburne
Painted about 1767
Oil on canvas, 50 x 40"
Amelia B. Lazarus Fund, 1923

⊰6⊱

BENJAMIN WEST, 1738-1820
The Return of the Prodigal Son
Painted about 1771
Oil on canvas, 54½ x 60⅛"
Maria De Witt Jesup Fund, 1923

❴ 24 ❵
CHESTER HARDING, 1792-1866
Mrs. Thomas Brewster Coolidge
Painted about 1828-1830
Oil on canvas, 36¼ x 28″
Rogers Fund, 1920

❦(2 5)❦

CHARLES CROMWELL INGHAM, 1796-1863
Amelia Palmer
Painted about 1830
Oil on canvas, 67⅞ x 53-9/16″
Gift of Courtlandt Palmer, 1950

❖{ 1 7 }❖

GILBERT STUART, 1755-1828
George Washington
The Phillips-Brixey Portrait
Oil on canvas, 29 x 23¾″
Bequest of Richard de Wolfe Brixey, 1943

❖19❖

THOMAS SULLY, 1783-1872
The Student (Rosalie Kemble Sully)
Dated 1839
Oil on canvas, 23½ x 19½″
Bequest of Francis T. S. Darley, 1914

⇥{ 26 }⇤

WILLIAM JAMES HUBARD, 1807-1862
Charles Carroll of Carrollton
Painted about 1830
Oil on wood, 18¾ x 14½″
Rogers Fund, 1956

❦ { 27 } ❦

SAMUEL LOVETT WALDO, 1783-1861
General Andrew Jackson
Painted about 1819
Oil on canvas, 25¾ x 21″
Rogers Fund, 1906

❧ 38 ❧
THOMAS COLE, 1801-1848
The Mountain Ford
Dated 1846
Oil on canvas, 28¼ x 40-1/16″
Bequest of Maria De Witt Jesup, 1915

⊰ 39 ⊱
ASHER BROWN DURAND, 1796-1886
The Beeches
Dated 1845
Oil on canvas, 60⅜ x 48⅛"
Bequest of Maria De Witt Jesup, 1915

⋊{ 28 }⋉

SAMUEL LOVETT WALDO, 1783-1861 and WILLIAM JEWETT, 1795-1873
The Knapp Children
Painted about 1850
Oil on canvas, 70 x 57½"
Gift of Mrs. John Knapp Hollins, in memory of her husband, 1959

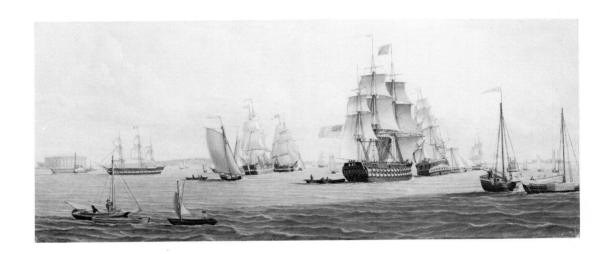

✦〔 29 〕✦
THOMAS THOMPSON, 1775/76-1852
Scene from the Battery, with a Portrait of the Franklin, 74 Guns
Painted about 1838
Oil on canvas, 30 x 65″
Bequest of Edward W. C. Arnold, 1954

❧(45)❧
ALBERT BIERSTADT, 1830-1902
Merced River, Yosemite Valley
Dated 1866
Oil on canvas, 36 x 50″
Gift of the Sons of William Paton, 1909

❧〔30〕❧
REMBRANDT PEALE, 1778-1860
George Washington
Oil on canvas, 36 x 29″
Bequest of Frances Mead, 1926

◄{ 31 }►
REMBRANDT PEALE, 1778-1860
Martha Washington
Oil on canvas, 36 x 29″
Bequest of Frances Mead, 1926

❧{ 32 }❧

WASHINGTON ALLSTON, 1779-1843
The Spanish Girl in Reverie
Painted in 1831
Oil on canvas, 30 x 25"
Gift of Lyman G. Bloomingdale, 1901

⊰{ 33 }⊱
HENRY PETERS GRAY, 1819-1877
The Wages of War
Dated 1848
Oil on canvas, 48¼ x 76¼"
Gift of Several Gentlemen, 1873

⊰ 34 ⊱

JOHN JAMES AUDUBON, 1785-1851
Ivory-billed Woodpeckers
Oil on canvas, 39¼ x 26¼″
Rogers Fund, 1941

≫{ 35 }≪
THOMAS HEWES HINCKLEY, 1813-1896
Rabbit Hunting
Dated 1850
Oil on canvas, 40 x 54¼″
Gift of Mrs. F. Livingston Pell, 1943

≫{ 36 }≪
ROBERT HAVELL, JR., 1793-1878
View of the Bay and City of New York from Mountain House, Weehawken
Dated 1840
Oil on canvas, 24 x 33″
Bequest of Edward W. C. Arnold, 1954

⊰ 37 ⊱
THOMAS COLE, 1801-1848
Landscape—The Fountain of Vaucluse
Dated 1841
Oil on canvas, 69 x 49⅛″
Gift of William E. Dodge, 1903

❖{40}❖

ASHER BROWN DURAND, 1796-1886
High Point: Shandaken Mountains
Dated 1853
Oil on canvas, 32¾ x 48″
Bequest of Sarah A. Ludlum, 1877

⊰41⊱
JOHN FREDERICK KENSETT, 1816-1872
The Old Pine, Darien, Connecticut
Painted about 1872
Oil on canvas, 34⅜ x 27¼"
Gift of Thomas Kensett, 1874

❧(42)❧

GEORGE LORING BROWN, 1814-1889
View at Amalfi, Bay of Salerno
Dated 1857
Oil on canvas, 33¼ x 53¾"
Gift of William Church Osborn, 1903

◦❨43❩◦
JASPER F. CROPSEY, 1823-1900
Mt. Chocorua, New Hampshire, Autumn
Oil on canvas, 28½ x 35½"
Painted about 1870
Bertram F. and Susie Brummer Foundation, Inc., Gift, 1961

▸⟨ 44 ⟩◂

WORTHINGTON WHITTREDGE, 1820-1910
The Trout Pool
Dated 1870
Oil on canvas, 36 x 27⅛″
Gift of Col. Charles A. Fowler, 1921

>|(46)|<

THOMAS MORAN, 1837-1926
The Teton Range
Dated 1897
Oil on canvas, 30 x 45″
Bequest of Moses Tanenbaum, 1937

≥{ 47 }≥
WILLIAM KEITH, 1839-1911
Approaching Storm
Dated 1880
Oil on canvas, 30 x 50″
Gift of Mrs. Scott Scammell, 1951

⊁{49}⊰

MARTIN JOHNSON HEADE, 1819-1904
Hummingbird and Passionflowers
Oil on canvas, 20 x 12″
Gift of Albert Weatherby, 1946

◆{ 51 }◆

SEVERIN ROESEN (died about 1871)
Still Life: Fruit
Dated 1855
Oil on canvas, 36 x 50″
Rogers Fund, 1963

❧ 52 ❧
DAVID GILMORE BLYTHE, 1815-1865
Corn Husking
Painted about 1850-1855
Oil on canvas, 24 x 33½"
Catherine Lorillard Wolfe Fund, 1957

❧{ 53 }❧
EASTMAN JOHNSON, 1824-1906
Corn Husking at Nantucket
Painted about 1875
Oil on canvas, 27⅝ x 54¼″
Rogers Fund, 1907

◄{ 54 }►
EASTMAN JOHNSON, 1824-1906
The Funding Bill
Dated 1881
Oil on canvas, 60½ x 78¼″
Gift of Robert Gordon, 1898

⊰ 55 ⊱

THOMAS WATERMAN WOOD, 1823-1903
A Bit of War History: The Contraband, The Recruit, and The Veteran
Dated 1866
Oil on canvas, each 28¼ x 20¼"
Gift of Charles Stewart Smith, 1884

❧(56)❧

JOHN GEORGE BROWN, 1831-1913
Meditation
Oil on canvas, 30 x 25"
George A. Hearn Fund, 1909

⟨ 57 ⟩

HENRY MOSLER, 1841-1920
Just Moved
Dated 1870
Oil on canvas, 29 x 36½″
Arthur H. Hearn Fund, 1962

⊰ 59 ⊱
EDWARD LAMSON HENRY, 1841-1919
Old North Dutch Church
Dated 1869
Oil on millboard, 18 x 14″
Bequest of Maria De Witt Jesup, 1915

❧ 61 ❧

HENRY ALEXANDER, 1860-1895
The Laboratory of Thomas Price
Painted about 1887
Oil on canvas, 36 x 30″
Alfred N. Punnett Endowment Fund, 1939

{ 62 }

FREDERICK REMINGTON, 1861-1909
Cavalry Charge on the Southern Plains
Dated 1907
Oil on canvas, 30⅛ x 51⅛"
Gift of Several Gentlemen, 1911

❦{ 63 }❦
THOMAS HOVENDEN, 1840-1895
The Last Moments of John Brown
Dated 1884
Oil on canvas, 77⅜ x 63¼"
Gift of Mr. and Mrs. Carl Stoeckel, 1897

✧❨64❩✧

ROBERT F. BLUM, 1857-1903
The Ameya—A Japanese Candy Vendor
Painted about 1890
Oil on canvas, 27⅜ x 31″
Gift of the Estate of Alfred Corning Clark, 1904

⊰{ 66 }⊱
WINSLOW HOMER, 1836-1910
The Veteran in a New Field
Dated 1865
Oil on canvas, 24 x 38″
Lent by Adelaide Milton de Groot, 1952

❧(67)❧

WINSLOW HOMER, 1836-1910
Cannon Rock
Dated 1895
Oil on canvas, 39-3/16 x 39⅛″
Gift of George A. Hearn, 1906

⟪ 69 ⟫
THOMAS EAKINS, 1844-1916
Arcadia
Painted about 1883
Oil on canvas, 38¾ x 45½″
Lent by Adelaide Milton de Groot, 1952

◦{ 70 }◦

THOMAS EAKINS, 1844-1916
Signora Gomez d'Arza
Painted in 1901-1902
Oil on canvas, 30 x 24″
George A. Hearn Fund, 1927

❊ 71 ❊

WILLIAM MICHAEL HARNETT, 1848-1892
The Banker's Table
Dated 1877
Oil on canvas, 8⅛ x 12⅛″
Elihu Root, Jr., Gift Fund, 1956

{ 48 }

FREDERIC EDWIN CHURCH, 1826-1900
The Parthenon
Dated 1871
Oil on canvas, 44-3/16 x 72⅛"
Bequest of Maria De Witt Jesup, 1915

◄ 50 ►

JAMES PEALE, 1749-1831
Still Life: Balsam Apple and Vegetables
Oil on canvas, 20¼ x 26½"
Maria De Witt Jesup Fund, 1939

❪ 72 ❫
JOHN FREDERICK PETO, 1854-1907
Office Board
Dated 1885
Oil on canvas, 23½ x 19½"
George A. Hearn Fund, 1955

᚛ 73 ᚜

JOHN QUIDOR, 1801-1888
The Wall Street Gate
Dated 1833
Oil on canvas, 27⅛ x 34⅜″
Gift of Roy Neuberger, 1961

≈{ 58 }≈

FRANK WALLER, 1842-1923
In the Metropolitan Museum, Cruger Mansion
Dated 1881
Oil on canvas, 24 x 20-1/16"
Purchase, 1895

⊰〔 60 〕⊱

JOHN FERGUSON WEIR, 1841-1926
Forging the Shaft
Painted in 1877
Oil on canvas, 52-1/16 x 73¼″
Gift of Lyman G. Bloomingdale, 1901

❖⟨ 74 ⟩❖
ELIHU VEDDER, 1836-1923
Roman Girls on the Seashore
Dated 1877
Oil on canvas, 18¼ x 58¾"
Arthur H. Hearn Fund, 1958

❧ 75 ❧

RALPH ALBERT BLAKELOCK, 1847-1919
A Waterfall, Moonlight
Painted before 1886
Oil on canvas, 56¼ x 36″
Bequest of Eda K. Loeb, 1952

⊰{ 66 }⊱

WINSLOW HOMER, 1836-1910
Snap the Whip
Dated 1872
Oil on canvas, 12 x 20″
Gift of Christian A. Zabriskie, 1950

❋(68)❋
THOMAS EAKINS, 1844-1916
Pushing for Rail
Dated 1874
Oil on canvas, 13 x 30-1/16″
Arthur H. Hearn Fund, 1916

⊱⟨76⟩⊰
ALBERT PINKHAM RYDER, 1847-1917
Toilers of the Sea
Painted before 1884
Oil on wood, 11½ x 12″
George A. Hearn Fund, 1915

◆⟨ 78 ⟩◆

UNKNOWN HUDSON VALLEY PAINTER
Young Lady with a Rose
Dated 1732
Oil on canvas, 32½ x 27″
Gift of Edgar William and Bernice Chrysler Garbisch, 1962

ALBERT PINKHAM RYDER, 1847-1917
Forest of Arden
Finished in 1897
Oil on canvas, 19 x 15″
Bequest of Stephen C. Clark, 1960

Above, below, where'er the astonished eye
Turns to behold, new opening wonders lie,

With uproar hideous first the *falls* appear,
The stunning tumult thundering on the ear.

This great o'erwhelming work of awful Time
In all its dread magnificence sublime,

Rises on our view, amid a crashing roar
That bids us kneel, and Time's great God adore.

18   25

◦{ 83 }◦
EDWARD HICKS, 1780-1849
The Falls of Niagara
Dated 1825
Oil on canvas, 31½ x 38″
Gift of Edgar William and Bernice Chrysler Garbisch, 1962

❯79❮
RUFUS HATHAWAY, 1770?-1822
Lady with Her Pets
Dated 1790
Oil on canvas, 34¼ x 32″
Gift of Edgar William and Bernice Chrysler Garbisch, 1963

◆{ 80 }◆

ERASTUS SALISBURY FIELD, 1805-1900
Ellen Tuttle Bangs
Painted about 1838
Oil on canvas, 58¼ x 30″
Gift of Edgar William and Bernice Chrysler Garbisch, 1963

Attributed to JAMES PEALE, 1749-1831
Washington Reviewing the Western Army at Fort Cumberland, Maryland
Painted about 1795
Oil on canvas, 22¾ x 37¼"
Gift of Edgar William and Bernice Chrysler Garbisch, 1963

‹{ 82 }›
FREDERICK KEMMELMEYER (active 1788-1803)
The American Star
Painted about 1800
Oil on paper, 22 x 17¾"
Gift of Edgar William and Bernice Chrysler Garbisch, 1962

≈{ 84 }≈

JAMES G. EVANS (active 1827-1854)
The Tow Boat Conqueror
Dated 1852
Oil on canvas, 40 x 50″
Gift of Edgar William and Bernice Chrysler Garbisch, 1962

❦{ 8 5 }❦

UNKNOWN PAINTER
Burning of the Sidewheeler Henry Clay
Painted about 1852
Oil on canvas, 36 x 54¼"
Bequest of Edward W. C. Arnold, 1954

⇥⟨ 86 ⟩⇤

JOHN CARLIN, 1813-1891
After a Long Cruise
Dated 1857
Oil on canvas, 20 x 30″
Maria De Witt Jesup Fund, 1949

◦⟨ 88 ⟩◦

WILLIAM MERRITT CHASE, 1849-1916
Still Life: Fish
Oil on canvas, 40⅛ x 45″
George A. Hearn Fund, 1908

⊷〖 90 〗⊷

WILLIAM MORRIS HUNT, 1824-1879
Sandbank and Willows
Oil on canvas, 24 x 42″
Gift of Francis M. Weld, 1938

✦⟨91⟩✦

WILLIAM MORRIS HUNT, 1824-1879
The Bathers
Painted in 1878
Oil on canvas, 38 x 25″
Morris K. Jesup Fund, 1936

◆{ 92 }◆

JOHN LA FARGE, 1835-1910
Bishop Berkeley's Rock, Newport
Dated 1868
Oil on canvas, 30¼ x 25¼"
Gift of Frank Jewett Mather, Jr., 1949

⊰｜93｜⊱

SAMUEL COLMAN, 1832-1920
Defending the Cup
Dated 1870
Oil on canvas, 30-3/16 x 60⅛"
Arthur H. Hearn Fund, 1962

⟨ 94 ⟩
ALEXANDER H. WYANT, 1836-1892
An Old Clearing
Dated 1881
Oil on canvas, 49¼ x 37"
Gift of Robert Gordon, 1912

❋{ 95 }❋
HOMER DODGE MARTIN, 1836-1897
Harp of the Winds: A View on the Seine
Dated 1895
Oil on canvas, 28¾ x 40¾"
Gift of Several Gentlemen, 1897

⊁⟨97⟩⊰
GEORGE INNESS, 1825-1894
Spring Blossoms
Dated 1889
Oil on canvas, 30¼ x 45¾″
Gift of George A. Hearn, in memory of Arthur Hoppock Hearn, 1911

{ 98 }

JAMES ABBOTT McNEILL WHISTLER, 1834-1903
Cremorne Gardens, No. 2
Painted about 1875
Oil on canvas, 27 x 53⅝″
Kennedy Fund, 1912

◄〖99〗►

JAMES ABBOTT McNEILL WHISTLER, 1834-1903
Harmony in Yellow and Gold: Connie Gilchrist, The Gold Girl
Painted about 1876-1879
Oil on canvas, 85¾ x 43⅛″
Gift of George A. Hearn, 1911

J. H. SCHENCK (active about 1860)
Third Avenue Railroad Depot
Oil on canvas, 36¼ x 50¼″
Bequest of Edward W. C. Arnold, 1954

◆{ 102 }◆

MARY CASSATT, 1845-1926
Mother and Boy, Painted about 1902
Oil on canvas, 32⅛ x 25⅞″
The H. O. Havemeyer Collection
Bequest of Mrs. H. O. Havemeyer, 1929

⊰{ 103 }⊱
JOHN SINGER SARGENT, 1856-1925
The Lady with the Rose—Charlotte Louise Burckhardt
Dated 1882
Oil on canvas, 84 x 44⅜″
Bequest of Mrs. Valerie B. Hadden, 1932

❧{ 89 }❧

WILLIAM MERRITT CHASE, 1849-1916
The Hall at Shinnecock
Painted about 1895
Oil on canvas, 40⅛ x 35″
Amelia B. Lazarus Fund, 1913

❧ 105 ❧
JOHN SINGER SARGENT, 1856-1925
Alpine Pool
Painted about 1912
Oil on canvas, 27½ x 38″
Gift of Mrs. Francis Ormond, 1950

{ 106 }
CECILIA BEAUX, 1855-1942
Mr. and Mrs. Anson Phelps Stokes
Painted about 1898
Oil on canvas, 72 x 40″
Gift of the Family of the Rev. and Mrs. Anson Phelps Stokes, 1965

✦100✦

THEODORE ROBINSON, 1852-1896
Giverny: Bird's-Eye View
Dated 1889
Oil on canvas, 26 x 32¼″
Gift of George A. Hearn, 1910

❈{ 101 }❈

MARY CASSATT, 1845-1926
Portrait of a Young Girl
Painted about 1900
Oil on canvas, 29 x 24⅜″
Anonymous Gift, 1922

⇥107⇤

CHILDE HASSAM, 1859-1935
Union Square, New York, Dated 1890
Oil on canvas, 18⅛ x 18⅛″
Gift of Miss Ethelyn McKinney
in memory of her brother, Glenn Ford McKinney, 1943

⊰108⊱

CHILDE HASSAM, 1859-1935
Isles of Shoals
Dated 1901
Oil on canvas, 25 x 30″
Gift of George A. Hearn, 1909

◆❨104❩◆

JOHN SINGER SARGENT, 1856-1925
Edward Robinson
Dated 1903
Oil on canvas, 56½ x 36¼″
Gift of Mrs. Edward Robinson, 1931

◈⟨113⟩◈
KENYON COX, 1856-1919
Augustus Saint-Gaudens
Dated 1908
Oil on canvas, 33½ x 46⅞″
Gift of Friends of the Sculptor, 1908

❦ 109 ❧

JULIAN ALDEN WEIR, 1852-1919
The Red Bridge
Painted about 1896
Oil on canvas, 24-3/16 x 33¾″
Gift of Mrs. John A. Rutherfurd, 1914

✦｛ 110 ｝✦

JOHN HENRY TWACHTMAN, 1853-1902
Horseneck Falls
Oil on canvas, 30 x 25″
Lent by Adelaide Milton De Groot, 1952

❧〔119〕❧

WILLIAM GLACKENS, 1870-1938

Central Park in Winter

Painted about 1905

Oil on canvas, 25 x 30″

George A. Hearn Fund, 1921

THOMAS WILMER DEWING, 1851-1938
Green and Gold
Oil on canvas, 24¼ x 22½″
Gift of Elisabeth Ball, 1953

⊰112⊱

GEORGE De FOREST BRUSH, 1855-1941

Allen Harriman

Dated 1905

Oil on canvas, 56¾ x 39-5/16″

Gift of General Boykin C. Wright, 1953

❧{114}❧

JAMES J. SHANNON, 1862-1923
Magnolia
Dated 1899
Oil on canvas, 71¾ x 39⅛"
George A. Hearn Fund, 1913

THOMAS POLLOCK ANSHUTZ, 1851-1912
The Cabbage Patch
Dated 1879
Oil on canvas, 24 x 17″
Morris K. Jesup Fund, 1940

⊶116⊷

ROBERT HENRI, 1865-1929
Dutch Girl in White
Painted in 1907
Oil on canvas, 24 x 20″
Arthur H. Hearn Fund, 1950

◄{ 117 }►

GEORGE LUKS, 1867-1933
The Old Duchess
Dated 1905
Oil on canvas, 30 x 25″
George A. Hearn Fund, 1921

‣❴118❵‣

JOHN SLOAN, 1871-1951
Dust Storm, Fifth Avenue
Dated 1906
Oil on canvas, 22 x 27″
George A. Hearn Fund, 1921

❧❨120❩❧
ARTHUR B. DAVIES, 1862-1928
Adventure
Painted about 1910
Oil on canvas, 18⅜ x 30⅛″
Bequest of Miss Lizzie P. Bliss, 1931

◆⟨ 1 2 1 ⟩◆

ARTHUR B. DAVIES, 1862-1928
Italian Hill Town
Oil on canvas, 25⅞ x 39⅞″
Bequest of Miss Lizzie P. Bliss, 1931

◆{ 1 2 2 }◆

MAURICE PRENDERGAST, 1859-1924
Group of Figures
Oil on canvas, 23¼ x 27½″
Lent by Adelaide Milton de Groot, 1952

≫〔 1 2 3 〕≪

ERNEST LAWSON, 1873-1939
Winter
Painted in 1914
Oil on canvas, 25 x 30⅛″
George A. Hearn Fund, 1915

◆｛124｝◆
GEORGE BELLOWS, 1882-1925
Tennis at Newport
Painted in 1919
Oil on canvas, 40¼ x 43¼″
Lent by Adelaide Milton de Groot, 1952

⭑|125|⭑

GIFFORD BEAL, 1879-1956
The Albany Boat
Dated 1915
Oil on canvas, 36⅜ x 60¼"
George A. Hearn Fund, 1917

❧ INDEX TO PLATES ❧

◄(COLOPHON)►

35,000 copies

Printed: June 1966 by Diablo Press, Berkeley, California

Typography: 9 point and 11 point Monotype Perpetua

Typographer: Vernon Simpson typographers Inc., Los Angeles, California

Designer: Louis Danziger, Los Angeles, California